NEALE LECTURE IN ENGLISH HISTORY
1973

The Fame of
Sir Thomas Gresham

S. T. BINDOFF

JONATHAN CAPE
THIRTY BEDFORD SQUARE LONDON

The Fourth Neale Lecture in English History
was delivered on December 6th, 1973
at University College, London

© 1973 by S. T. BINDOFF

JONATHAN CAPE LTD
30 BEDFORD SQUARE, LONDON WCI

ISBN 0 224 00928 1

PRINTED IN GREAT BRITAIN
BY EBENEZER BAYLIS AND SON LTD
THE TRINITY PRESS, WORCESTER, AND LONDON

THE FAME OF SIR THOMAS GRESHAM

THOMAS GRESHAM may have been a great Elizabethan, but his ghost belongs among the eminent Victorians. It is only since the last century that his name has become, if not a household word, at least one to conjure with in market-place and council-chamber. It had never, of course, been forgotten – he had seen to that with his calculated investment in immortality. Yet when, two hundred years or more after his death, the centrepiece of that design, his College and Lectures, had been allowed to rot almost away, the memory of its fashioner might likewise have faded from minds unlearned or uncommitted.

From any such lapse into oblivion it was to be saved by a twist of fate. In 1836 an enlightened Lord Mayor offered a prize for an essay on Gresham's life and character. The winner was a 23-year-old named John William Burgon, who before reluctantly entering his father's failing business had spent a year at the University of London, that is to say, at this College, where he had also carried off an essay prize. Balked of the prospect of seeing his Gresham essay in print, he had laid it aside when in January 1838 the Royal Exchange was burnt to the ground. Public interest in its founder at once revived, Burgon was spurred on to expand his little essay into a big book, and in August 1839 there appeared the two volumes of the *Life and Times*. 'Gresham', observed its author, as he put the finishing touches, 'may think himself lucky to have been the subject of a *young* author's *opus magnum*.' He was right: the book was to become not only his own monument – a perfect line of poetry apart – but one of its subject's also.[1] For Gresham, however, the fire was to do yet more. By depriving his Lectures of both income and lodging – they had been housed in the Exchange since 1768 – it forced the hand of authority in the vexed question of their future, and in 1843 they moved into their first purpose-built home, the new Gresham College in Basinghall Street. When in the following year Queen Victoria revived memories of 1571 by opening the present Royal Exchange, both institutions had been given a new look.

So, too, had the shade of their founder. In 1845 Gresham became the first Londoner to be commemorated in the City by a modern street-name. (It was a wry coincidence that two of the lanes eventually so rechristened had been previously known as 'Lad' and 'Maiden', for Gresham, we recall, was a man with a roving eye.) Businessmen were quick to rally. Already in 1843, on the demise of the City of London Commercial Club, its successor was styled The Gresham, a name, to quote the club's centennial history, 'honoured since Elizabethan days in the City'. Four years later Jacob Unwin introduced steam-power into his printing works in Bucklersbury and renamed it 'The Gresham Steam Press'. So far as I know, he was first in the field, but he was followed within the year by the Gresham Life Assurance Society, and then in quick succession by other firms. Today there remain a dozen within the City and twice that number in Greater London which owe this nominal allegiance: they include a second insurance company and four others concerned with money or property, while among the miscellaneous remainder are a wine store and a pen company, suitable progeny for one who was a great consumer of both.[2]

No other London worthy approaches Gresham's popularity as a commercial patron. In so far as City folk, in the flush of their ascendancy, felt the need of a tribal hero, they found him in the great Elizabethan. And it was because he already stood so high that his myth was to receive its greatest addition. In 1857 Henry Dunning Macleod let loose, under the title of Gresham's Law, the fable that he was the first to have explained why bad money drives out good. Despite the swift refutation of the claim (which Macleod later accepted), a hungry public swallowed it whole, and by 1912 the *Dictionary of National Biography* had to concede that the term was 'universally adopted by writers on currency'. Today his Law remains the one thing that everybody knows about Gresham who knows anything about him at all.[3]

The close of the century all but saw his apotheosis. Into the history of the civil war which nearly destroyed the University of London in the 'eighties and 'nineties I must resist the temptation to diverge. The rebels, those who fought for a 'professorial' or 'teaching' university separate from the institution then bearing the name, came nearest to victory in the autumn of 1891 when their draft charter seemed on the point of acceptance by the Privy Council. There remained, however, one difficulty, the name to be given to the new establishment. First entitled 'The Albert University of London', it had been shorn of the geographical suffix to prevent confusion, only to meet the objection that the name Albert *tout seul* would be insufficient. To this problem a solution was forthcoming from a different quarter. In February 1892 the Joint Grand Gresham Committee, the body which administers the Trust for the City Corporation and the Mercers' Company, resolved that Gresham College should co-operate with the new university provided it was renamed 'The Gresham University'. The offer, which included the use of the College lecture-hall as a senate house, was blessed by *The Times* and accepted by the petitioners, and it was under the banner of the grasshopper that they fought the next, and last, battle of their campaign. Its setting was a Royal Commission, the Gresham University Commission, and it ended in their defeat. Guerilla operations were to continue for some time, but it was Union, in the form of a reconstructed University of London, that triumphed over Secession, and Gresham who beat a retreat to his modest establishment in Basinghall Street.[4]

This set-back apart, it went on being a success story. If time allowed, and perception sufficed, I might try to catch some of its nuances. The name itself, in its succinct and sturdy Englishry: Palavicino, Burlamachi, they had stolen no soul away! And after the name, the face: leaving the iconography to Dr Roy Strong, we might yet reflect that to have been painted by Anthony Mor was no bad bid for immortality. By one test alone – but it is the ultimate one – the Gresham myth must be found wanting. What staid Victorians called the 'foolish stories' told about him are either patently borrowed or in other ways unmemorable. Gresham's grasshopper is no match for Whittington's cat.[5]

It was towards the end of the year 1551 that Thomas Gresham first moved centre-stage in Tudor history.[6] He was then about thirty-three years of age. The second son of Sir Richard Gresham, he had been educated at St Paul's and at Gonville Hall, Cambridge, and had then spent eight years as an apprentice mercer to his uncle, Sir John. In 1543, shortly after becoming free of his trade, he married a fellow-mercer's widow, a union which helped towards his admission, at Easter 1544, to the livery of the Company. For the next five years, until his father's death, he was occupied in business on his own account but under older eyes. Two years more and he entered the service of the Crown.[7]

Predestination was at work here – not to speak of Original Sin. The Greshams came from Norfolk, where besides the village which gave them their name, and perhaps their punning family sign, the name is borne by the school at Holt founded by Sir John; but their spiritual home was the City of London. Commercial success brought in its train not only civic eminence – Sir John and Sir Richard both served as Lord Mayor – but also entanglement in public finance, especially during the orgiastic fifteen-forties; and it was as both a stalwart and a creditor of his king that Sir Richard obtained those huge grants of monastic land, including Fountains, which put him high among the commoner-beneficiaries of that great share-out.

The Greshams were businessmen to whom court feuds and factions were matters for insurance: theirs was the *politique du florin*, and it meant staying near the centre of power. The client first of Wolsey and then of Thomas Cromwell, Sir Richard shifted his allegiance after 1540 to the rising house of Seymour.

One of Thomas Gresham's sisters married Edward Seymour's factotum John Thynne; his brother John fought with the Protector at Musselburgh and received his knighthood on the field; and Sir Richard himself in his will, made early in 1549, named Somerset first among a long list of recipients of rings. One naturally wonders whether that doomed ship carried Gresham money: the presumption is that it did.[8]

It was under Somerset that Thomas Gresham played his first name-part in the melodrama of mid-Tudor public finance, but it was Somerset's victorious rival Northumberland who put this promising junior on the road to stardom. Gresham was to prove himself adept at surviving changes of régime, and this his first transfer of allegiance – the grasshopper's first jump – was predictable. The loosening of political and social discipline which bedevilled Somerset's protectorate could not have pleased the Greshams, least of all when their own shire was rocked by the earthquake of 1549. When in that August John Dudley went to Norfolk on his bloody mission, it was the Gresham house at Intwood which served as his first headquarters. A couple of months later Sir John Gresham was one of the city magnates who witnessed the fallen Protector's melancholy passage through London to the Tower; and if, as is likely enough, his ex-apprentice nephew was at his side, that young apostle of success would have needed no Polonian prompting to draw the prudent moral.[9] When, two years later, Somerset's career ended on Tower Green, his own began at Antwerp: in January 1552 he went there as Royal Agent.

The post of Royal Agent, or King's Merchant, was the resultant of two forces, the financial exigencies of the English government, and the pre-eminence of the Antwerp money-market. Both had begun to operate during the early part of the sixteenth century, but it was only after 1540 that they came fully into play; they remained so for a quarter of a century, after which they rapidly diminished. These twenty-five years were the heyday of the Royal Agency, and they were conterminous with its exercise by two able men, Stephen Vaughan, who held it under Henry VIII, and – after an unsatisfactory interlude – Thomas Gresham, who filled it almost continuously from 1551 to 1574. The Agent's principal task was to negotiate the loans of which the English government stood in constant and sometimes desperate need, and which the Antwerp bankers were alone capable of furnishing. Thus there came to prevail between London and Antwerp in the mid-sixteenth century a relationship comparable with that obtaining between London and New York four hundred years later; and one hopes that in due course Gresham was able to welcome to the Celestial Bourse – for he would not have left the Heavenly City unprovided with that amenity – his latter-day successor, Lord Keynes.[10]

The handling of the Crown's business at Antwerp involved periodic rather than continuous duties, and neither Vaughan nor Gresham was permanently domiciled in that city, although Gresham always kept a factor there to deal with both official and private business. Taking the fifteen years from his first mission in January 1552 until his last in March 1567, I estimate that he spent in all about six years abroad, and this total includes a mission of several months to Spain in 1554–5. He appears to have spent about twice as much time at Antwerp under Edward VI and Mary as under Elizabeth. Incidentally, the record of his missions provides a simple test of his numerical reliability, something that matters a good deal to the student of his career. In 1563 he supported a plea to Elizabeth for some reward for his labours with the statement that he was then engaged upon his twenty-fourth journey overseas since her accession: by my reckoning it was his eleventh. Three years later he similarly multiplied, or transposed, his thirteenth journey into his thirty-first. (If he was reckoning two crossings to each mission, he was being disingenuous.) It is fair to add that his still more startling claim to have posted at least forty times between Antwerp and 'the Court' during his two years' (really eighteen months') service under Edward VI, which all writers from Burgon onwards have treated as Channel crossings (at a rate of one double crossing every other week!), clearly refers instead to his frequent journeys from Antwerp to Brussels.

The intermittent character of Gresham's service at Antwerp raises two questions. The first is, how was he remunerated? The answer is that he was not, at least not directly. From first to last Gresham received no salary. He was given his 'diet', that is, a subsistence allowance, at the rate of twenty shillings a day, and he also drew something for his staff and for other expenses, including entertainment. Apparently down to 1563 Elizabeth paid him his pound a day the whole year round, but in that year she limited it to his sojourns abroad. As these were becoming rarer and briefer, the restriction was not unreasonable, but Gresham took it hard. In lieu of salary he did receive, after the fashion of the time, grants of land from the Crown. We have his own statement—it appears, for a change, to have been an understatement—that between them Edward and Mary gave him lands worth £300 a year. Elizabeth's contribution was, predictably, smaller: down to 1572 we hear of only two grants amounting to £27 a year, and those after persistent solicitation.[11]

Before lapsing into sarcastic comment on the Queen's valuation of years of expert and resolute service, we should ask whether he had not offset it by taking steps to remunerate himself. If by this euphemism we mean, did he defraud his employers? then I think that the answer must be, in general, no. Whether we are disposed to add the rider that it was not for want of trying will depend, in the first instance, upon what we make of his accounts and of their reception by their auditors. Best known, because it was recounted by Hubert Hall nearly a century ago, is the story of how the reception of his last account in 1574 was followed by his dash to Kenilworth to secure the Queen's remission of a deficit of £10,000 established against him. In extenuation of what has usually been seen as a sizeable blot on an otherwise clean sheet it has been argued that the government was itself to blame for not having called him to account earlier (his last discharge dated back eleven years) and that the amount in dispute represented less than two per cent of the total under review. Yet Hubert Hall had himself prefaced his account of this episode by an analysis of the transactions of the years 1558 to 1563, from which, he concluded, Gresham had emerged with a 'surplus' of £3,000, while alongside this can be set the aftermath of Gresham's fingering of part of the 'Spanish treasure' of 1568, his admission that he could not find a sum of £4,000 owing to the Queen and his offer in its stead of two manors which had fallen to him as security for an unredeemed loan.[12]

In these cases, as in others, the discrepancies arose in large part from Gresham's claims for allowances. The sixteenth century had no monopoly of disputed expense accounts, but the operations in which Gresham was engaged, and the circumstances surrounding them, were bound to provoke such argument. The root of the trouble was the capacity in which he expected, and was expected, to serve. Was he the Crown's agent in the sense that he did its business on a non-profit basis, or was he allowed to make a profit, and if so how, and how much? Was, for instance, the brokerage appearing in the accounts — although never, so far as I know, mentioned in his terms of engagement — due to him as middleman between the Crown and its creditors, or to the intermediaries between him and them, or to both?[13] If such questions seem hard to answer, what is plain is that there were less crude ways open to Gresham of turning his official position to private advantage than simply 'cooking the books'. In becoming the Royal Agent he did not cease to be a businessman, and his two hats were interchangeable. His native wit, backed by his lineage, had got him the appointment, but his retention of it under successive rulers owed much to his advance in wealth, prestige and connections. As his own credit grew, he was more often called upon to employ it for his sovereign. When the private banker was at the beck and call of the Royal Agent, the Agent could scarcely have been expected to cold-shoulder the banker. At different times Gresham held large sums of money on Crown account, and it is not to be doubted that he used it in private transactions, or that in many other ways his own business benefited from his official position, inside knowledge and strategic contacts.[14]

However well or ill rewarded in his lifetime, Gresham's services have been rated high by posterity. Not only is he commonly accorded a large share of the credit for bringing England, alone among the major European states, through the perilous 'fifties and 'sixties without a financial breakdown, but he is also held to have done so through an understanding of the behaviour of money unprecedented in a native of these islands and unsurpassed by any of his foreign contemporaries. That England did survive the crisis, that the Antwerp loans were indispensable to the outcome, and that these loans were always forthcoming, not seldom on better terms than the rulers of the Netherlands could command – these are facts which cannot but reflect credit on the man who for fifteen years had the handling of these great affairs. But the question is, how much credit? We cannot doubt his own answer: it was that of the Tower Bridge policeman to the old lady who asked him which was the Bloody Tower – 'All of it, madam, all of it.' For whatever Gresham's qualities, modesty was not among them. His letters are one long voluntary upon his own trumpet: and as there are over three hundred of those letters the resulting blast is well sustained. That it has carried across the centuries will not surprise us when we remember how much easier it is to accept his version, particularly since so much that he wrote has been so long in print, than to search elsewhere. His full, and often dramatic, narratives of his bargainings with the princes of the Bourse, his reports on the eccentricities of the market, his denunciations of those at home, especially the two Winchesters, the bishop and the marquess, who were frustrating his cleverest tricks, these and similar themes call for patient scrutiny before we can begin to say how far his version is from the facts.[15]

Two features of Gresham's operations as Royal Agent have attracted particular notice. They are his 'device' for using the Merchant Adventurers to sustain the exchange-rate during a refunding operation, and his plan for supporting the rate by what we may loosely call an exchange equalization account. Of the first, the clearest description was given by Mr Buckley fifty years ago. The essence of the scheme was the compulsory acquisition by the Crown from the Merchant Adventurers, under the threat of not allowing their cloth ships to sail to Antwerp, of a large slice of the proceeds of this cloth in foreign currency, and that at a rate more favourable than could be obtained in the market. As to the utility of the scheme to the Crown there can be no two opinions: indeed, so patently useful was it that, in a milder form, it dated back for at least a century. But as to its effect upon the exchange, opinions vary. We can, with Unwin, dismiss Gresham's own claim that, when used in the autumn of 1552, it raised the value of sterling by some thirty per cent as pure moonshine: if sterling made so marked a recovery at that time it was because the government had just called down its debased coins to half their nominal value, thus administering the first real check to the inflation which had accompanied the debasement. But whether the device either prevented the rate from falling or even helped to raise it slightly is a more open question: Buckley thought that it did not, De Roover that it may have done. I will make only two comments. First, I find it difficult to believe that this high-handed attempt to interfere with the price of sterling can have proved any more successful than simultaneous efforts to interfere piecemeal with the price of anything else. And second, I think that here, as elsewhere, what is needed is a little less theorizing and a few more facts. Herbert Spencer used to say that the greatest tragedy in life was a theory killed by a fact. If that is indeed so, then Clio must be, after all, the Tragic Muse.[16]

There is a good deal more to be said in praise of Gresham's other notion, the plan to support the exchange by official intervention. He first suggested this to Northumberland in August 1552, and for a short time during the autumn of that year he was given a weekly allowance of £1,200 with which to carry it out. Unfortunately the payments were soon suspended and the scheme lapsed. Whether it would have achieved anything – the rate was tending to rise at the time – is open to doubt; none the less, Gresham can be credited with a grasp of one of the techniques of modern exchange control, systematic intervention out of funds set aside for the purpose.

Just as it is no small part of the fascination of Gresham's performance that he doubled the roles of public servant and businessman, so his discharge of his official duty gains enormously in interest from the energy and ambition with which he strove to inflate it. The *Zeitgeist* was, of course, in his favour. One does not have to read much sixteenth-century history to be struck by its parallels with our own time: and in few respects is the resemblance more striking than in the scope which it gave to the experts in economics to throw their weight about. Such an opportunity the pundit of Antwerp could be trusted to seize, if not with both hands, then with the one that wielded his pen; and through screed after screed we can follow that correspondence course in Money which two queens and three secretaries of state received from the Lange Nieuwstraat. One at least of its recipients made the grade: in October 1559 Sir William Cecil was informed by his mentor that he was now a 'doctor' in exchange, a graduation which did not exempt him from the rigours of the post-doctoral course.[17]

No such ordeal awaits you, for into Gresham's exposition of the exchanges I shall refrain from entering: those who have sampled it will know, and those who have not can imagine, how fascinatingly repulsive a subject it is. I will pose, or rather repeat, one question only: did Gresham write the 'Memorandum for the Understanding of the Exchange', of which the late Raymond de Roover published a handsome edition – its twenty pages of text prefaced by a 280-page introduction – under the title 'Gresham on Foreign Exchange' and with the sign of the grasshopper on the binding? Both date and authorship of the document have since become the subject of learned debate.[18] I will only rush into this and out again. If we accept De Roover's – and some others' – dating of the treatise, it must have been written within a short time of Gresham's well-known and clearly authentic letter of 1558 to Elizabeth. In that case, if he had written both, we should expect some resemblance. But what we find is that both documents, after expository portions which reveal little similarity, conclude with recommendations which not only do not resemble each other but differ in such a way as to make it all but incredible that the same man wrote both. The Memorandum has fourteen recommendations, the letter five: no single one is common to both sets.

We shall do better to base our judgment of Gresham upon his known writings. To me, at least, these prove that he was one whom Nature had endowed with a practical flair but with no matching gift of explaining it. Such born manipulators owe nothing to analysis: all that the great Maurice Tate could say of one of his most fearsome deliveries was, 'I grips her in my hand and I lets her go.' Gresham took much longer to say little more. Yet he had his flashes of illumination. The man who could tell Cecil in 1563 that £20,000 worth of saltpetre would be better store than £100,000 worth of gold and silver had, as we might say, got something there.[19] And his letter of 1558 to Elizabeth, after an orgy of mis-statement and special pleading, ends with a five-point programme, four of whose items – an honest currency, few debts, few licences or exemptions, and the faithful performance of bargains – should figure in any list of the golden rules of public administration.[20]

It was the mid-'sixties which saw the real end of Gresham's career as Royal Agent, although he retained the status and discharged the duties until 1574. We have seen that his missions abroad became less frequent after 1563 and came to an end in 1567. His reluctance to go on his travels again may have owed something to the lameness caused by his falling from a horse and breaking a leg in 1560. His frequent complaints of this disability and of his loss of vigour should, however, be treated with caution, for as late as 1577, when it was a question of lading shot for Barbary, he was mobile enough;[21] but he had lived strenuously, he had earned some ease, and his life had been clouded by the death of his son, his only legitimate child, in 1563.

It was not only Gresham who was changing, it was the world in which he had grown up and passed the prime of his life and career. The centre of Gresham's world was Antwerp, and in the fifteen-sixties Antwerp was feeling the first spasms of a long-drawn-out agony. To that disaster we must not overlook our own country's contribution. The quip of the time that if Englishmen's fathers were hanged at Antwerp's gates their sons would come creeping back between their legs at once expresses and obscures a truth. For the story of the English connection with Antwerp is the story of the husband and wife who cannot live apart but who have difficulty in living together. Down to 1560 the lady's charms had never failed to recapture her spouse after every quarrel. But thereafter the old magic lost its power: perhaps it was the course of rejuvenation which the gentleman went in for just about that time. For this new, this rejuvenated, England, the England of Elizabeth and Cecil, seemed bent on loosing itself from a connection which, once the sheet-anchor of the nation's security, now felt more like a millstone round its neck. Which way the wind was blowing was shown by a tiny straw. Early in 1564 Gresham reported that the Antwerp magistrates had made him a gift of forty shillings'-worth of wine, the first *douceur* he had received in his thirteen years' official association with the city; to him, as to us, it was an ominous sign.

No one of Gresham's temperament and outlook could have come to know Antwerp so intimately without wanting to see his own land adorned by such a jewel. This was the vision which inspired the first of his two civic benefactions, his Burse. London already had a money-market, but it was an open-air one: it was, literally, the 'street', that is, Lombard Street. What Gresham did was to give this market a local habitation in the shape of a faithful copy of the Antwerp Bourse: and what

Elizabeth did was to give it a name, the familiar name of the Royal Exchange. It is an oft-told tale, and it might be left there but for a couple of reflections. To Charles Macfarlane, writing an unfashionably critical biography in 1845, the Burse represented 'not the munificence of a donor, but the calculation of a projector and capitalist'. And he was not far wrong. For if Gresham put up the building, the City and citizens of London had bought the land, at a cost of over £3,000.[22] Yet it was Gresham who drew the rents from the shops which overlooked the quadrangle and the vaults which lay beneath it. At first slow to let at 40s. a year, the shops benefited from the Queen's visit and were soon fetching up to 90s.; by 1596 the yearly revenue was £730. The cost of the building we can only guess at, but if we put it at the same figure as for the land, a yield of £500 per annum during Gresham's last years would have represented a return of some eight per cent on the combined investment or of double that rate on his own share of it. The price of civic fame has not always been so reasonable.

Then there is the curious incident of the Queen's bestowal of the new name. To a later age, more accustomed to such tokens of majesty's favour, this could not but appear a signal honour done to the man and the institution. So it may have been, but was it only that? Gresham's Burse was a monument to the enterprise of a city and a citizen; it owed nothing to initiative or support by the government. It was modelled on and named after the Bourse of Antwerp, another municipal institution, and one, moreover, exempt from all but the lightest control by higher authority.[23] Yet the London Burse was designed to foster a branch of commerce, the trade in bills of exchange, over which the English Crown had long claimed, and from time to time had sought to wield, a control based on prerogative and sanctioned by statute. There was, indeed, an office, *Cambium Regis* or Exchange Royal, through which this control might be exercised, and in 1575 it was given to none other than the Lord Treasurer. Burghley's appointment was to be followed, eighteen months later, by yet another effort to institute a licensing system: this was announced in a proclamation which opened with the reminder 'that by the laws and statutes of this realm no man ought to make any exchange or rechange of money but such as her majesty shall authorize, or their lawful deputies', and went on to vest this authority in three London merchants. If this was the official line in 1576 may we not take it to have been so five years before? When, on that January afternoon, the Queen 'caused the same Burse by an herald and a trumpet to be proclaimed the *Royal Exchange*, and so to be called henceforth, and not otherwise', it was, I venture to suggest, in obedience to her instinct to defend the royal prerogative in all its branches.[24]

It is taken for granted that Gresham rendered a valuable service to London through his share in the foundation of the Exchange. Yet the nature of that service is hardly made clear, and it is indeed not easy to determine. That the institution became instantly popular as a rendezvous, shopping precinct, news centre, amusement arcade, even football stadium, to all this there is no lack of witness.[25] But it was not to cater for these things—the profitable shops apart—that Gresham had built it: he wanted merchants and their money, merchants of all nations and bills on every market. It is unlikely that they ever came in the numbers and variety he hoped for. London's trade and finance were not, to anything like the extent of Antwerp's, handled by foreigners who periodically descended on the city and could not do without such a meeting-place. The Exchange could never hope to attain to the international status of its prototype. What it could do, and did, was to provide an overwhelmingly native body with facilities not readily accessible before. Easily first among these was insurance, which settled in from the outset and has become identified—one could almost say synonymous—with the Royal Exchange ever since.[26] If it ousted St Paul's as the customary place for the discharge of debts, for their contraction the new centre was never to compete with the separate establishments which clustered around it. The rise of English banking owed little or nothing to the

Exchange, and the nation's financial centre still goes under the name of the street which the Burse was meant to supplant.[27]

Gresham was allowed rather less than ten years during which to enjoy the reflected glory of the Exchange as well as the more tangible rewards of his strenuously successful pursuit of success. He was by now established in his mansion in Bishopsgate, which he had bought after being given his knighthood in 1560. And forth from that efficient manufactory the money flowed in many directions. Some of it returned to acquire yet more of the soil of East Anglia, and to Intwood there was added another fair house at Ringshall in Suffolk. Some went south into Sussex, where the estate at Mayfield which he had taken over from his less fortunate cousin Sir John – whom Thomas had not emulated in his perhaps too expensive hobby of sitting in Parliament – became one of Gresham's favourite retreats as well as the headquarters of his considerable interest in the iron industry. But it was in West Middlesex, much patronized by Court and City, that he lavished most of his care and money upon the great house at Osterley where, in due course, he entertained his sovereign.[28]

By the middle 'seventies Gresham had few worlds left to conquer. He turned, as did so many of his contemporaries and successors from the ranks of big business, to that world of the mind from which his own world, the world of getting and spending, had long seduced him. When he made his will in 1575 it contained a bequest for further education. He passed over the universities, including his own college which its master was re-founding with money made in London and which was to attract much more support from that city. Instead, he went in for the novelty of a college in London itself. As Fuller put it, having already established a kind of college for merchants, he now founded a kind of Exchange for scholars. Why he did so, and why on its idiosyncratic pattern, remains something of a mystery even after the recent focusing of interest on the early fortunes of the institution. Unlike the Exchange, the College took shape only after Gresham's, and his widow's, death, and what the Trustees, under pressure from all sides, made of it is no sure guide to its founder's motives or intentions. Any influence from abroad, whether Antwerp or elsewhere, is hard to discern, while the projects of Nicholas Bacon and Humphrey Gilbert, both members of his circle, have little in common with his College save their London location. That decision has been held to reflect, besides civic loyalty, an enthusiasm for learning on the 'new model', as has the choice of some of the seven subjects to be lectured on. That the lectures were to be available to all cannot but appeal to a generation which has produced its own Open University.[29]

Ideas may be weighed, but money can be counted, and we are on surer ground with the business side of the bequest. This fell under two heads, the gift of Gresham House as the college building and of the Exchange as the source of the endowment. A building and an endowment — what more could any college ask for, then or now? Only, perhaps, that the bequest might have been more generous in scale and less rigid in form. The house was valued at £66 13s. 4d. a year and the seven lecturers were to receive £50 a year apiece, a total of £416 13s. 4d. If, to make comparison easy, we capitalize this at five per cent, it approaches £8,500. Among similar benefactions, the two London examples, Matthew Sutcliffe's ill-fated college at Chelsea and Thomas White's more fortunate Sion, both dating from a generation later, were to account for £16,000 and £6,000 respectively. At Oxford Sir Thomas Pope's Trinity had cost him £5,000 and Sir Thomas White's St John's over £13,000; and at the end of the century Sir Thomas Bodley was to spend over £8,000 on his library and, with his friends, a further £11,000 on its stocking and furnishing. Even a selection of such rough totals shows that Gresham's benefaction was not an exceptionally large one.[30]

He could have afforded more. Gresham often passes for the richest commoner of his day, but this he certainly was not: Thomas Sutton, his junior by fourteen years, was both a far wealthier man and a much greater giver. Yet Gresham was not poor. He left real estate—the evidence about his personal property is meagre—worth £2,670 a year or in capital value more than £50,000. Of this the College was to receive, at his widow's death and initially for fifty years, about one-sixth. It was not all that much more than the £280 a year which went to his illegitimate daughter Anne, the wife of Nathaniel Bacon, or the provision for his servant-girl, Anne Hurst, by whom he had a son when nearing sixty, the boy himself and the father Gresham found for him. It was less than one-third of what his widow was to have for transmission to her descendants.[31] If, as was noted at the time and has often been repeated, Gresham Lecturers were to be paid more than Regius Professors, the foundation as a whole was not outstanding in its munificence, especially as the money was really not all Gresham's to give. As we have seen, the Exchange which provided the income had cost his fellow-Londoners perhaps as much as it had cost him. That would have mattered less if he had given the College the whole of the revenue from the Exchange and thus the possibility of a rising income; but the amount was fixed from the start, and although some of the surplus was to assist the College, in the upkeep of the house for instance, this was not laid down in the will.[32] It was perhaps a reflection of these anomalies that, almost alone among the educational foundations of the age, Gresham College was to attract no supplementary legacies: Londoners great and small would go on fostering other academies, but not the one which has always been looked upon as peculiarly their own.

The position with regard to the house was different. That was Gresham's to give and he gave it in its entirety. Even allowing for the cost of its upkeep, it was an asset of immense potential value. Its subsequent neglect was shameful and its eventual surrender a catastrophe. I leave it to those among my audience versed in such things to attach a rental to 50,000 square feet fronting on Old Broad Street for which the Treasury continues to pay the £500 a year fixed in 1767.[33]

*

None of this could Gresham have foreseen. What he bequeathed was a house which, once he quitted it, would cease to be the hub of a great mercantile enterprise. It was in the kitchen of that house, early in the evening of Saturday, November 21st, 1579, that on coming home from the Exchange he suddenly fell down, 'and being taken up, was found speechless, and presently dead'.

NOTES

1. E. M. Goulburn, *John William Burgon ... A Biography* (1892), vol. I, p. 110. The quality of Burgon's book owed something to his friendship with Patrick Fraser Tytler, with whom he worked among the State Papers in 1838 and whose memoir he was to write twenty years later; Tytler's *England under the Reigns of Edward VI and Mary* also appeared in 1839.
2. *The Gresham Club Centenary, 1843–1943*, p. 3; *Unwins: A Century of Progress ... 1826–1926*, p. 26; *Post Office Telephone Directory Section 102* (1972), p. 322. For the story of the sign of the grasshopper at 68 Lombard Street see G. Chandler, *Four Centuries of Banking, as illustrated by ... the constituent banks of Martins Bank Limited*, vol. I (1964), p. 41 and pl. 21; the present grasshopper dates from 1930.
3. Macleod suggested the term in *Elements of Political Economy* (1857), p. 477, half acknowledged its inappropriateness in *The Theory and Practice of Banking* (3rd edn., 1875), vol. I, p. 120, and did so fully in *The History of Economics* (1896), p. 38, adding unrepentantly that it had been universally accepted.
4. For a contemporary narrative, see W. H. Allchin, *An Account of the Reconstruction of the University of London*, 3 parts (1905–12), and for a recent survey, see H. Hale Bellot in *The Victoria County History of Middlesex*, vol. I (1969), pp. 324–8. The name had first been suggested by Professor Warr of King's College in a letter to the Selborne Commission of 1888; its revival in 1892 followed the abandonment of a proposal that Gresham College should become a constituent of the new university (*Gresham University Commission ... Report ... 1894* [C.–7259], p. 426), an arrangement envisaged from the outset of the campaign (University of London Library. Association for Promoting a Teaching University for London. Reports and

Papers. Letter of June 11th, 1884, announcing first meeting). For a similar suggestion by a Charity Commission Inspector in 1857, see *Notes, Evidences, and Suggestions relating to Gresham College*, pp. 29, 39, 59–60. Within the last decade the Lectures have become associated with The City University, and the College building now houses the university's Graduate Business Centre; see P. Winckworth, *A History of the Gresham Lectures: An Inaugural Lecture ... 14 July 1966.*

5. Some of the stories are, however, of respectable antiquity, like that of the drinking of the pearl, which forms an incident in Thomas Heywood's play 'The Second Part of If you know not me, you know no bodie' (1606), in *Two Historical Plays of the Life and Reign of Queen Elizabeth*, ed. J. P. Collier for the Shakespeare Society (1861), p. 119. For the possible origin of another story, and its unexpected sequel, see *Notes and Queries*, vol. CLXV (1933), p. 248.

6. The difficulty of dating with any precision Gresham's inauguration as Royal Agent is reflected in the conflicting statements on the point by modern writers. The post was not an office to which its holder was formally appointed, and the only account of its conferment on Gresham appears to be his own in his memorandum of (?) August 1553 (Burgon, vol. I, pp. 115–120). Weighing the — not wholly consistent — statements in this version with the circumstantial evidence, I am inclined to choose October 1551. Although the Day Book (see note 7) furnishes no decisive clue, it includes references to a visit to court with other merchants (no. 6481, October 20th), a comprehensive audit of Gresham's books (no. 6491, November 6th) and his purchase of a new house in Eastcheap (nos. 6524–5, November 25th).

7. The uniquely important source for Gresham's career during these years is his Day Book, extending from 1546 to 1552, preserved at Mercers' Hall. This was analysed by Mr (now Professor) Peter Ramsey in his unpublished doctoral thesis, and is described in his essay 'Some Tudor Merchants' Accounts', in *Studies in the History of Accounting*, ed. A. C. Littleton and B. S. Yamey (1956), pp. 185–201. Extracts from the Day Book appear in G. Chandler, *Four Centuries of Banking*, vol. I, pp. 26–31. The Book is not paged or foliated, but its 6569 entries are numbered continuously and are so cited here.

8. The Day Book records various transactions with Somerset:

nos. 4508–9 (June 10th, 1549), 4623 (purchase of armour, July 2nd, 1549), 4902 (gift of two 'apes' of silver, September 4th, 1549) and 6147 (debt to Gresham £102 1*s.* 5*d.*, February 18th, 1551). It was Sir Richard's money-lending as well as his land-grabbing which seem to have provoked the satirical 'epitaphium' on him: see A. G. Rigg, 'Two poems on the Death of Sir Richard Gresham (ca. 1485–1549)', *Guildhall Miscellany*, vol. II (1967), pp. 389–91.

9. An entry in the Day Book (no. 4987) reveals that Gresham visited Windsor on October 8th, 1549, the day before Somerset surrended to Northumberland. Was he an emissary, perhaps with his friend Hoby, or did he go privately, in the hope maybe of helping Thynne, who was there with Somerset? The *coup d'état* has been most recently described in W. K. Jordan, *Edward VI: The Young King* (1968), pp. 506–23.

10. For the extensive literature of the relationship, and of its English and Netherlands settings, see C. Read, ed., *Bibliography of British History: Tudor Period 1485–1603* (2nd. edn, 1959), esp. pp. 246–58; M. Levine, *Tudor England 1485–1603* (Conference on British Studies Bibliographical Handbooks, 1968), esp. pp. 47–57; and the bibliographies in O. de Smedt, *De Engelse Natie te Antwerpen*, vol. I (1950), pp. 8–41, vol. II (1954), pp. 727–731, and in H. van der Wee, *The Growth of the Antwerp Market and the European Economy* (3 vols., 1963), vol. I, pp. xxxiii–lix. The most illuminating study of the Antwerp loans is R. B. Outhwaite, 'The trials of Foreign Borrowing: the English Crown and the Antwerp Money Market in the Mid-Sixteenth Century', *Economic History Review*, 2nd ser., vol. XIX (1966), pp. 289–305, and the most important recent contribution is J. D. Gould, *The Great Debasement* (1970), esp. pp. 87–113. A comprehensive study by Dr G. D. Ramsay is in the press.

11. Gresham mentioned the figure of £300 in his letter of October 3rd, 1563, to Elizabeth (*Calendar of State Papers, Foreign*, 1563, p. 537; Burgon, vol. II, p. 39), whereas the grants as enrolled were valued at £365 2*s.* 7*d.*; perhaps he scaled them down because they were reversions (*Calendar of Patent Rolls*, 1553, p. 240; 1553–4, pp. 260–61; 1555–7, pp. 152–4; see also Burgon, vol. I, pp. 111–12, 189–90).

12. H. Hall, *Society in the Elizabethan Age* (3rd edn, 1902), pp. 63–9, 160–62; *Historical Manuscripts Commission, Salisbury*, vol. I (1883), pp. 573–5.

13. For the heavy cost of such allowances, including brokerage, successfully claimed by Gresham, see Outhwaite, *loc. cit.*, p. 303, n 1.

14. For a glimpse of the reverse situation, in which the Crown owed him money, see *Calendar of State Papers, Foreign*, 1566-8, p. 351.

15. The first essential, however, is a complete edition of the letters to replace the haphazard, and sometimes tendentious, selections in Burgon and in J. M. B. C. Baron Kervyn de Lettenhove and L. Gilliodts van Severen, *Relations politiques des Pays-Bas et de l'Angleterre sous le règne de Philippe II* (11 vols., 1882–1900), and the abridgments in the Calendars of State Papers and the Reports of the Historical Manuscripts Commission. The promised publication, within two or three years, of such an edition, now being prepared by Dr G. D. Ramsay, will be the greatest event in Gresham studies since 1839. Dr Ramsay generously put his transcripts at my disposal during my preparation of this lecture.

16. H. Buckley, 'Sir Thomas Gresham and the Foreign Exchanges', *Economic Journal*, vol. XXXIV (1924), pp. 589-601; R. H. Tawney, ed., *Studies in Economic History: the Collected Papers of George Unwin* (1927), 150-57; R. de Roover, *Gresham on Foreign Exchange* (1949), 218-25. De Roover's argument is criticized by Outhwaite, *loc. cit.*, pp. 299-300 and n 2.

17. *Calendar of State Papers, Foreign*, 1559-60, p. 68.

18. Mary Dewar, 'The Memorandum "For the Understanding of the Exchange"; its Authorship and Dating', *Economic History Review*, 2nd ser., vol. XVII (1964-5), 476-87; S .E. Lehmberg, 'Gresham, Mildmay, and the Memorandum for the Understanding of the Exchange', *Notes and Queries*, vol. CCVI (1961), pp. 403-405; D. R. Fusfield, R. de Roover, 'On the Authorship and Dating of "For the Understanding of the Exchange" ', *Economic History Review*, 2nd ser., vol. XX (1967), pp. 145-52; J. D. Gould, *The Great Debasement*, pp. 161-4. Dr C. E. Challis has kindly shown me an unpublished article of his own on the subject in which, drawing on his profound knowledge of the currency history of the period, he concludes in favour of the dating first suggested by De Roover but leaves open the question of authorship.

Dr Challis has also advised me on another aspect of Gresham's reputation which I have regrettably had to omit from my sketch, namely, his alleged influence on the English recoinage. Dr Challis confirms my own view that there is little or no foundation for the often sweeping claims of such influence, which are usually based on nothing more than his inclusion of a plea for a sound currency in his letter of 1558 to Elizabeth, a plea which many of his contemporaries would have made. I have also to thank Professor R. Tittler, the biographer of Nicholas Bacon, for confirmation of this view.

19. *Calendar of State Papers, Foreign*, 1563, p. 239.
20. The original of this celebrated letter, which Burgon printed from a transcript made by John Ward and inserted in Ward's own copy, now in the British Museum, of his *Lives of the Professors of Gresham College* (1740), is among the Harley (alias Portland) Papers (vol. I, fol. 83) at Longleat; see *Historical Manuscripts Commission, Bath*, vol. II, p. 16. It appears to have been first identified by J. E. Jackson in 1872: see *Notes and Queries*, 4th ser., vol. X, p. 70.
21. At the end of the Day Book, among pages left unused when the continuous entries ceased to be made in 1552, are notes, in Gresham's hand, of a series of payments in April and May 1577 mostly relating to the transaction mentioned in the text and including the cost of a night-ride to the Isle of Wight, where the ship concerned lay. These notes appear to furnish the last evidence we possess of Gresham's business activities.
22. The City also provided 100,000 bricks: see R. R. Sharpe, *London and the Kingdom* (3 vols., 1894–5), vol. I, p. 498 and n 6.
23. J. Denucé, 'De Beurs van Antwerpen: Oorsprong en eerste ontwikkeling, 15e en 16e eeuwen', *Antwerpsch Archievenblad*, 2de reeks, 1931, pp. 81–145.
24. The Exchange Royal was first described in *Cambium Regis, or the Office of His Majestie's Exchange Royall* (1628); the best modern account is in the introduction to Thomas Wilson, *A Discourse upon Usury (1572)*, ed. R. H. Tawney (1925), esp. pp. 138–53. For the episode of 1575–6, see C. Read, *Lord Burghley and Queen Elizabeth* (1960), pp. 145–6, and P. L. Hughes and J. F. Larkin, eds., *Tudor Royal Proclamations*, vol. II (1969), no. 618. For the Queen's visit, see John Stow, *A Survey of London*, ed. C. L. Kingsford (new impr., 1971), vol. I, p. 193. In the French edition (1582) of his description of Antwerp, the last which he revised, Guicciardini wrote that the Queen had renamed the Burse 'afin qu'il ne se reportast au modelle &

exemple de la Bourse d'Anvers', but added that such was the familiarity of the old name that it was still in daily use: *Description de la Cité d'Anvers*, ed. M. Sabbe (1920), p. 41. The name continues to appear, for example in plays, for a generation or more.

I am grateful to Miss Jean Imray, Archivist to the Mercers' Company, for giving me the benefit of her own studies of the early history of the Exchange, and for help in many other ways.

25. Much of it is collected in Burgon, vol. II, pp. 504–508; for football, see Sharpe, *op. cit.*, vol. I, p. 502 and n 2.

26. H. E. Raynes, *A History of British Insurance* (2nd edn, 1964), esp. chap. iii.

27. For a reflection of the continuing prestige of Lombard Street in the phraseology of policies, see F. Martin, *The History of Lloyd's* (1876), p. 32.

28. The stables are the only substantial part of Gresham's house to survive: *Historical Monuments Commission: Middlesex* (1937), pp. 74–5 and pl. 148.

29. Among many recent works, Joan Simon, *Education and Society in Tudor England* (1966) and W. H. G. Armytage, *Civic Universities* (1955) survey the general and university scene, and Christopher Hill, *Intellectual Origins of the English Revolution* (1965) explores the 'modernity' of the early Gresham College. A detailed study of the College down to 1660 is in preparation by Mr Ian Adamson of St John's College, Cambridge, who has kindly indicated to me the trend of his conclusions.

30. W. K. Jordan, *The Charities of London 1480–1660* (1960), pp. 252–67.

31. *An Exact Copy of the Last Will and Testament of Sir Thomas Gresham Kt.* (1724), pp. 27–31; for the case of Anne Hurst, see *Calendar of State Papers, Domestic*, 1595–7, pp. 328–9.

32. In March 1597 the City and Company estimated their outgoings under all heads at £862 a year, of which the upkeep of the Exchange and Gresham House accounted for £258 13s. 4d.; in addition, the two buildings needed £300 spent on their repair: Acts of Court of the Mercers' Company 1593–1629, fols. 14–14v.

33. E. Featherstone, *Sir Thomas Gresham and his Trusts* (1952), p. 12.